Also by Bill Bryson

THE LOST CONTINENT
MOTHER TONGUE
NEITHER HERE NOR THERE
MADE IN AMERICA
A WALK IN THE WOODS

NOTES from a SMALL I